STINGERS

STINGERS

BILL GUNSTON

Foreword by JACK KRINGS, chief test pilot,

McDonnell Douglas Corporation

HAMLYN

First published in 1990 by The Hamlyn Publishing Group,
a division of The Octopus Publishing Group Ltd
Michelin House, 81 Fulham Road, London SW3 6RB

Photographs: © McDonnell Douglas, except as below

Additional photographs are by © George Hall/Check Six, p15, 19, 20-21, 88-89,
104-105, 106-107; Nigel Bradley p140-41 and Canadian Armed Forces p133-139.
Thanks also to Geoffrey Norris, McDonnell Douglas, Europe,
Tim Beecher, Director of Communications, McDonnell Douglas Corporation, St Louis, Miss
and Captain Yves Generoux, Canadian Armed Forces Europe.

Typeset by SX Composing Ltd, Rayleigh, Essex

ISBN 0600 568 261

Produced by Mandarin Offset
Printed and bound in Hong Kong

FOREWORD

I remember November 18, 1978 well. I was sitting inside the F/A-18 for the first time spooling it up to military power. I took off from about 2000 feet of runway and the flight lasted about fifty minutes.

At the end of that flight I felt pleasantly surprised by the way in which the test had gone. It was at that moment I had a gut feeling that the plane I was test flying would end up as the best all round fighter in the Western armory. I am now convinced that this is true.

Along the way there were some problems – which is normal – but somehow nothing seemed to be an insuperable problem. It is a tribute to all those persons who were involved in developing the program and making it a reality.

It gives me particular pleasure to front this book which shows like none before it the power and grace of the plane in superb photography and words the F/A-18's development, from its early experimental days thru to todays operational squadron status.

Jack Krings
St Louis, Miss.

INTRODUCTION

Most fighter pilots are proud of the aircraft they fly, and confidently declare that they would expect to win in whatever combat situation they found themselves. But the Hornet is rather special.

It is a fighter. It is also an attack aircraft. In fact it was the first aircraft ever designed to be equally good at both missions. It can also quickly be converted into a multisensor reconnaissance aircraft. It can also operate from an aircraft carrier. It was also designed from the start to use radar-guided, medium-range, air-to-air missiles for stand-off interceptions.

With such versatility it is small wonder that its pilots are impressed, even though it is not a particularly large, powerful or fast aircraft. It just happens to be an outstanding all-rounder. To quote two Hornet pilots:

'It's a superbly designed airplane for the single-piloted mission' (US Marine Corps).

'When I strap into that cockpit I feel like there's nothing I can't do' (US Navy).

In the early 1970s the US Air Force was studying the potential of a lightweight fighter (LWF). It did not necessarily intend to buy any LWFs, but merely wished to discover whether such an aircraft could fly useful missions. Two types of LWF took part in a fly-off competition, one being the Northrop YF-17.

In 1974 the US Navy obtained Congressional approval to carry out a similar exercise and study a VFAX (fixed-wing fighter attack experimental). The Navy was concerned at the high price of the large and very capable F-14 Tomcat, and wanted to see whether a cheaper aircraft could be designed that could replace the F-4 Phantom in the fighter role and the A-7 Corsair in the attack role.

Of course, such an aircraft could have been designed, but later in 1974 Congress terminated the VFAX programme, and instead directed that the Navy should investigate suitably adapted versions of the US Air Force LWF prototypes. This directive could easily have led to a disastrous situation, such as that which occurred during 1963-68 with the futile attempts to build a Navy fighter version of the Air Force TFX (F-111). Often a desire to save money turns out to be devastatingly expensive in both time and money. But on this occasion the result could hardly have been better.

McDonnell Douglas carried out a careful evaluation of the YF-17 and determined that it could be redesigned to meet the Navy's requirement. Externally the redesigned aircraft looked hardly altered, but inside it was very different. The greatest innovation was the decision to slice the fuselage down the centre and splice in an extra section in order to make it wider. At a stroke this roughly doubled the internal fuel capacity. Of course it also made the aircraft heavier, so the wing was enlarged. The combination of increased weight and suitability for carrier operation required a completely new landing gear of greatly increased strength, with a twin-wheel nose gear incorporating a catapult towbar and strange main gears whose wheels, carried on pivoted arms, would hang downwards on the approach and then rotate backwards as the aircraft settled down on the deck or runway. The wider fuselage made it easier to fit a multimode radar in an enlarged nose, and at the rear the engine bays, originally tailored to 15,000-lb General Electric YJ101 bypass turbojets, were slightly enlarged to accommodate 16,000-lb F404 turbofans from the same supplier. The wing was arranged to fold and a hook added. Later the horizontal tailplanes were redesigned and many other parts altered.

The original idea was to produce an F-18 fighter version and an A-18 attack version, but the differences were so minor (mainly confined to avionics) that, especially after the development of an outstanding one-man cockpit, it was found possible to launch production of a common aircraft, designated F/A-18. A further result was that Navy and Marine Corps squadrons equipped with the Hornet acquired completely new designators, VFA and VMFA respectively, denoting their unique capability of flying either a fighter mission or an attack mission – or, rather, of performing both tasks on the same mission!

Most of the engineering changes were made at McDonnell Aircraft at St Louis, home of the Phantom, Eagle and Harrier II. The design team also quickly developed a TF-18 Hornet trainer, with dual controls in a rear cockpit which replaced the forward fuselage tank, reducing internal fuel capacity by a mere 6 per cent. This aircraft was later redesignated F/A-18B. There was also a scheme for an RF-18 reconnaissance version, with the nose gun replaced by various reconnaissance sensors, but this was shelved for the time being.

McDonnell reached a teaming agreement with Northrop, under which the work and rewards were shared. Northrop's main contribution comprised the centre and rear fuselage and the sloping vertical tails, together with all the associated internal systems.

The first Hornet was rolled out from the St Louis plant on 13 September 1978, and it was first flown, by 'Jack' Krings, on 18 November of that year. Painted white, it had NAVY written on one side and MARINES on the other. On the whole the flight test programme went well, and the Hornet was the first aircraft to be developed under the Navy's Principal Site Concept, in which all prototypes and other development aircraft were, as far as possible, based not at the manufacturers but at the Navy Air Test Center at Patuxent (Pax) River.

Of course there were numerous difficulties, but nearly all were minor and quickly dealt with, only three being in any way serious. However, a fourth item, fighter mission takeoff weight, which was targeted at 36,000lb, actually started at 36,710lb and gradually crept higher, without anyone being especially worried. The three items that did matter were rate of roll, combat radius or range and carrier approach speed.

Roll rate was at first far below specification in major parts of the flight envelope, almost entirely because of lack of torsional stiffness in the wings. Accordingly, the wings were redesigned, with a new and much stiffer rear portion, combined with more powerful tailerons (powered tailplanes, which are the dominant roll control at high speeds). These, together with various other changes, including removal of the dogtooth on the leading flaps, resulted in a perfectly straight leading edge. When all these modifications had been carried through the rate of roll was generally adequate.

Range, or combat radius, was at first about 12 per cent below specification. It never quite reached the desired values, but most of the shortfall was made good by attention to many details, including fuel systems, engines and, above all, airframe design in order to reduce drag.

For carrier approach speed the Navy stipulated 125 knots (143 mph) with zero wind over the deck, but this was regarded as a maximum, 115 knots being the target to be aimed at. In fact the Hornet never got below 134 knots (154 mph) despite having exceptionally powerful high-lift devices, including full-span leading-edge flaps and colossal trailing-edge flaps which, together with drooped ailerons, give a high-lift cambered configuration from tip to tip. Per-

haps the most significant comment to be made on the approach speed is that the designated 134 knots has caused no significant problem in the first million flight hours.

One important factor in carrier landings – the only ones where the approach speed is of real significance – is that before engaging a wire the engines have to be at high power. In the case of an aircraft with augmented turbofan engines (equipped with afterburners) this usually means MIL or maximum dry power, in other words, the greatest possible power without the afterburners being in operation. This is because if no wire is caught, or if the hook or wire or anything else breaks, the aircraft must overshoot, and if the engines are not already at high thrust the aircraft will probably drop into the sea on going over the bows. Most engines take several seconds to spool up, and so the pilot must open the throttles well back on the approach, which makes the landing faster. The F404 engine accelerates with amazing rapidity, so it is safe to leave opening the throttles until the aircraft comes over the stern of the ship, approach speed thus remaining at the minimum value.

Another good feature of the General Electric F404-GE-400 engine is its very low idling thrust. This is a valuable quality in any combat aircraft, and especially in one which has to manoeuvre on crowded carrier decks. Despite this, slamming the power lever fully forward can provide full afterburning thrust in about four seconds. This is also extremely important in combat, though in fact the time taken to accelerate from Mach 0.8 to Mach 1.6 at 35,000 ft never did quite reach the 80 seconds stipulated by the Navy. The F-4J/F-4S Phantom takes about 120 seconds to do this. Early Hornets were disappointing, taking 165 seconds, but this time was gradually brought down to a little below that of the Phantom.

Another of the temporary problems resulted from the irresistible urge felt by squadron pilots to pull up to AOA (angle of attack) of around 90°. None of them had ever previously flown an aircraft in which such a thing was possible (though the F-14, with wings fully swept, can also reach very high angles). Of course, during the flight-test programme Hornets were flown into every kind of unnatural attitude, but once the aircraft reached the squadrons repeated excursions to AOA of about 90° resulted in severe, fluctuating side loads on the canted vertical tails, which soon began to suffer from fatigue damage at the roots. No fin was ever lost, and in fact the Hornet is designed to be flyable in this condition, but the damage would certainly have resulted in lost fins had the cracking been allowed to continue. The problem became really serious in August 1984, and McDonnell Douglas bore the cost of a modification programme which added 4-in steel doublers to two of the fin attachments and replaced a light fairing with a strong structural one. Modifications were introduced to aircraft on the assembly line at Northrop and, from November 1984, to aircraft already in service. Pilots are discouraged from exceeding AOA of 25° in the speed range of 300-400 knots in order to prevent a repetition of the problem.

Strangely enough, by 1984 the two principal manufacturers were locked in a bitter legal dispute. The author was retained as expert witness by Northrop in a battle over several aspects of the progamme. One problem was 'Who invented the Hornet?' In other words, was it a McDonnell Douglas aircraft or a Northrop aircraft? Again, Northrop was encountering severe difficulties in trying to market its own F-18L land-based version, which in theory seemed far superior to an aircraft burdened by the structure and equipment intended for carrier operation. Fortunately for some it was all settled out of court. McDonnell Douglas agreed in May 1985 to pay Northrop $50 million in return for becoming prime contractor for all existing and future versions of the Hornet. Despite its theoretically far superior performance the F-18L was dropped.

Thus all the export sales have been of a carrier-compatible aircraft made to nations that do not possess any aircraft carriers. The first such sale was of 114 CF-18As and 24 two-seat CF-18Bs to the Canadian Armed Forces in 1980. Canada is a bilingual country, and as 'Hornet' is a different word in French the name is not used at all (at least not officially) in the CAF. The CF-18s have a runway-type instrument landing system receiver, a powerful spotlight which can be shone from the left side of the fuselage for visually identifying intruding aircraft at night, and provision for carrying LAU-5003 pods for the high-velocity (4,920 ft/sec) CRV-7 rockets.

The next customer was the Royal Australian Air Force. The selection of the Hornet in preference to the rival F-16 was announced in Canberra on 20 October

1981, the deal being an exceedingly complex one. For an initial A$2,430 million (then equal to US$2,790 million) Australia was to receive 57 AF-18As and 18 two-seat ATF-18As, plus a lot of ground support (including complete buildings), but with Australian industry playing a significant role in the manufacture, assembly and test of the AF-18 and its F404 engine.

The third export customer was Spain, whose air force (Ejército del Aire) was to receive 72 aircraft, designated by McDonnell Douglas as 60 EF-18As and 12 two-seat EF-18Bs, and by the Ejército del Aire

as C.15s and two-seat CE.15s. The order was placed in May 1983, and contained an option for a further 12 aircraft, although the high unit price of $41.67 million for the main batch might discourage taking up this option. Again, Spanish industry plays a role, with offset manufacture of many major parts for all F/A-18s.

In mid-1989 the only other export customer was Switzerland. The air force (Flugwaffe) announced selection of the F/A-18 in October 1988. Though more expensive than its rival, the Hornet was described by the customer as 'a clear winner'. A total of 34 aircraft were required, including a few two-seaters. The deal will certainly include offset work for the Swiss aircraft industry.

Another country interested in the Hornet is South Korea. However, by autumn 1989 no decision had been announced by this potential customer.

Perhaps the maker's one regret is that the existence of such a versatile aircraft has an adverse effect on the number purchased. After all, there would be far more Hornets if the day fighter, night fighter, all-weather fighter, day-attack, night-attack, all-weather attack and reconnaissance versions were all separate aircraft instead of being combined in one!

Even eight of the oldest and most primitive Hornets, not suitable for shipboard operation, have been put to good use. Resplendent in blue and gold, they have since April 1987 equipped the US Navy's famed aerobatic display team, the Blue Angels. Equipped with smoke generators and special seat harness, they are unquestionably the best equipment this 'Flight Demonstration Squadron' has ever had.

Bill Gunston
September 1989

From the start we knew the Hornet was going to be a great airplane. In the matter of the cockpit, and especially the pilot displays, we were sure we were ahead of the world. In a few areas, such as drag and specific range, which is the distance you fly for burning a pound of fuel, we were marginally down at first, and we also had to do some major redesign of the wing to achieve the specified rate of roll, but throughout the whole flight-test program we always knew we were dealing with a great airplane. Once the wing had been stiffened rate of roll was no problem. The Hornet uses both ailerons and the horizontal stabilizers, or tailerons, to put on as much roll as the average pilot can take. We get particularly good feedback from the former attack pilots, who used to fly A-7s, and who are really impressed by how the Hornet can perform with a full load of bombs.

MCAIR design staff

In 1979 we learned a lot about the Hornet, nearly all of it good. From the start General Electric's F404 engine performed better than advertised. Idling thrust proved to be small, and spool-up acceleration absolutely out of this world, so that – though this is not by any means standard practice – we were able to demonstrate a waveoff with one engine at intermediate power and the other shut down! In early testing we discovered that the horizontal tails lacked sufficient power to raise the nose at speeds much below 140 knots, when the ideal would have been nearer to 100. The solution was to reprogram the software of the flight control system to turn both rudders 25° inwards. This gives a powerful down thrust on the tail which gets the nose gear off the deck at 115 knots, though of course the towbar pull is dominant until near the end of the catapult stroke. We also did many other things, including replacing the flattened oval section drop tanks, which were thought to be the optimum compromise between ground clearance and capacity, with simpler circular tanks which hold 330 US gallons compared with 300. At the end of the preliminary carrier suitability trials, flown from CV-66 *America* by Lt-Cdr Dick Richards and Lt Ken Grubbs, the Navy called this "The most successful sea trials in naval aviation history". I don't think any of us quite expected that.

Hornet design engineer

Toughest of the early shipboard tests were cat shots and arrested landings. The four catapults of *Carl Vinson*, each taking steam from the ship's nuclear-heated boilers, could fling a Hornet off the bows at full flying speed even if it had its jet engines switched off and the parking brake on!

Deck officer on the *Carl Vinson*.

Aircraft design is always a compromise. It would always be possible to make any aircraft *better*, but it would then cost more, be more complex to maintain and probably be less reliable. For example, while some fighters have complex engine inlet systems, with pivoting intakes and computer-controlled variable ramps and bleed doors in order to be able to work up to Mach 2 to 2.5, the Hornet has a simple inlet which is actually superior to the complex types most of the time, and is still good enough for a maximum speed of Mach 1.8.

Consultant design engineer

Out here on the range we know bombing accuracies better even than the pilots, and most Hornets score better in free-fall bombing than the A-7E, which we used to think tops. We use binoculars to see the tail codes. VW was the very first Marines unit, VMFA-314 "Black Knights", from El Toro. NK means VFA-25 "Fist of the Fleet", another local outfit.

NAS Fallon range officer

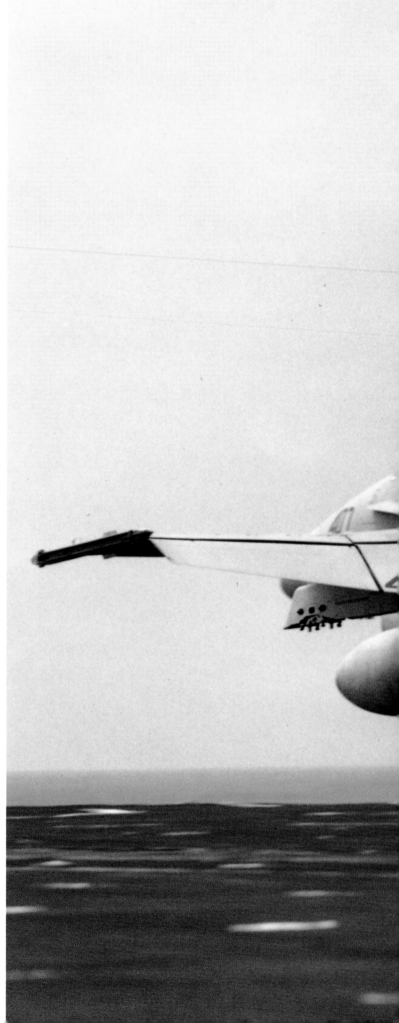

When McDonnell Douglas turned the YF-17 into the F/A-18 the outermost underwing stores pylons were omitted. In their place are fairings covering the aileron power units. However, the F/A-18 was equipped from the outset with attachments on the curved flanks of the fuselage, in recesses in the outer skin beside the engine air-ducts. Stores attached in these locations cause slightly less drag than those hung under the wings. The fuselage stations, called Nos 4 and 6, can carry Sparrow or AMRAAM air-to-air missiles. Alternatively they can be used for extra night/bad-weather sensors, a Flir (forward-looking infrared) and a laser spot tracker and strike camera.

MCAIR test pilot

Maximum external stores load is 17,000 lb, but on most training missions this limit is not even approached. The most common ordnance items, because they are the cheapest, are Mk 82 and Mk 84 bombs and rocket launchers. Other weapons include CBU-59 cluster bomblet dispensers, GBU-10 and -12 laser-buided "smart bombs", Maverick precision attack missiles – our Marines use the AGM-65E with laser guidance and a large 300-lb warhead, while the Navy is now introducing the AGM-65F anti-ship version with infrared homing – and the long-range AGM-84 Harpoon anti-ship cruise missile.

Ordnance officer

V FA-15 "Valions" was formerly VA-15, a light attack unit in the Atlantic Fleet equipped with the A-7E Corsair II. Today all the light VA squadrons in the carrier air wings have converted to the Hornet, changing their designator to VFA to signify their twin roles of fighter and attack. When you peel off to make a practice dive attack on a surface target using Mk 82 bombs, with Sidewinder missiles on their tip launching rails for self-defence against hostile aircraft.

F/A-18 pilot

Not having had to use it, the one thing I can say about the seat is that the Martin-Baker SJU-5 is real comfortable. But all of us are eager to get to know the next-generation NACES (Navy Aircrew Common Ejection Seat), the Martin-Baker Mk 14. This goes into the F/A-18C and D now coming off the line. We hear that sitting in this seat the pilot doesn't need to think much!

F/A-18 pilot

I love working topside, even in winter. It's kind of like a non-stop ballet performance, and being part of CV-64 *Constellation* I get to see it for nothing. Of course the cast dress for the part. I'm a grape; I wear purple, which shows I refuel the planes. The ordnance men like to think they're special, wearing red. Deck crews, tractor drivers for example, wear yellow. Catapult teams wear green. Everything has to be clean, like the Hornets.

US Navy deck crewman

The way a good ship works is like clockwork. Everyone knows exactly what to do. Like when a Hornet comes along we know his weight and dial it in so that the cat flings him off the bows at just the right speed. Here we're waiting a few seconds for the twin rams of the cat to return exactly to the launch point so we can couple up the towbar to Modex 406 from VFA-25. Then we tell him takeoff thrust, he raises his hand, the signal goes to the shooter and in two seconds he's off the ship.

Member of the greenjacket cat crew

I love to get up on deck now and then to watch the flying. The Hornets are different. In the sky and on deck they look what they are: mean, purposeful, supersonic fighters. On the approach they have giant flaps down and funny legs dangling, and they remind me of some kind of ungainly bird. Then they hit the deck and those legs just seem to fold up to make the "stinger" look mean and sleek again. I never tire of watching.

US Navy physician

If you live aboard for long you come to realize that even a giant supercarrier pitches and rolls quite severely at times. So even in good weather it's a rule that planes not wanted immediately are chained down. In the hangars you will find the same chain-down grid covering the floor as the one that covers the parking areas of the flight deck. Unlike some airplanes the Hornet folds just the wingtips before going down on the elevator. It's an easy airplane to spot, and the best plane to work on that most of us have met.

Member of hangar maintenance crew

We don't often fly with three tanks, and I've never heard of anyone making a carrier landing with three external tanks filled. To save money we tend always to bring them back to be used again, though if we were tasked to do an air combat mission against Top Gun F-16Ns we'd certainly not have tanks on. Empty tanks don't really affect performance all that much, and the approach is flown at the same speed and with the same excellent attitude which gives us a far better view ahead than most of us were used to. Just as you come in over the stern you go to MIL power, and the F404s hit that just about as you cross No 3 wire.

F/A-18 pilot

We're better at flying than writing, but lots of us mean to get round to writing to McDonnell Douglas. They have asked us to send in our impressions which they might use in their "Hornet Tales" advertising. Not many of us would disagree that we're all potential Hornet salesmen.

F/A-18 pilot

Familiarity breeds respect, in the knowledge that the F/A-18 does a pretty good job in both the fighter and the attack missions. . . . And it's getting better all the time, first with the F/A-18C/D and, later, perhaps with the proposed Hornet 2000.

F/A-18 pilot

We had had single TV-type colour displays in fighter cockpits previously, but the Hornet had not one but three. These replaced virtually all the traditional electromechanical (dial type) instruments, many of those remaining being merely standby instruments which, now that we have years of experience with the big displays, are generally seen to be unnecessary.

F/A-18 pilot

They offered me the chance to go back to another plane, but I didn't take it. No way. Once I strapped this plane on I didn't want to fly anything else. Right away I loved everything it gave me to work with: air-to-air, air-to-ground – all wrapped up in one tight little package.

F/A-18 pilot

A lot of the Hornet's sting is in the nose. The Hughes APG-65 radar was in 1979 one of the best multimode fighter radars in the world, with several advanced operating modes previously either never available at all or possible only with much bigger and heavier radars, which would have penalized the aircraft. Not least of the remarkable features of this radar is that it operates reliably despite being a few inches from the six muzzles of the M61 gun, blasting out 100 shots per second!

This, the standard gun of US fighters, is fed by a 570-round drum below the gun and immediately beind the radar. Those two prominent vents in the underside of the nose extract hot air and dangerous gas from the radar bay and the gun bay respectively.

USAF ground chief

L ike the F/A-18 the AGM-84 Harpoon is a product of McDonnell Douglas, and it is also fitted with wings and an air-breathing turbojet engine. Unlike the Hornet the Harpoon is designed to fly just one mission, but one which trades a small missile for a large ship. Harpoon's range is typically about 60 miles when air-launched, and suitable target ships can easily be seen and pinpointed at this distance by the Hornet's radar. Basic AGM-84 uses active radar to home on its target, but a later version, SLAM (Stand-off Land Attack Missile), has the imaging infrared seeker of one of the versions of Maverick, also carried by the Hornet.

Nobody today is greatly bothered about the Hornet's shortfall in range. In any case, cruise missiles such as Harpoon go some way towards making up for any deficiency.

MCAIR consultant engineer

I'm coming into the target area now, doing about 500 knots right on the deck. Eight kilometres out I pull my nose up about 45 degrees. Right then I spot a bogie. He's up there circling the target at about 10, maybe 15 thousand feet. I hit the button and immediately I'm air-to-air as I pull up to greet him.

A little thumb action and I've got it locked up. I shoot off a heat seeker – and nail him! Still have the mission to complete so I switch back to air-to-ground. I pull upside down, roll over and come in at about 45 degrees, drop my bombs – bull's eye! What a show. In one precise, fluid motion I'd gone from air-to-ground to air-to-air and back again. I've got a dead bogie and my bombs off – double trouble for the bad guys from one pilot, one plane. It's only taken a few seconds and virtually no effort. It couldn't be easier.

F/A-18 pilot

Great, but this does rather assume a pretty pathetic enemy, unable to nail a hostile aircraft climbing from sea level to about 15,000 feet and then unable to get him on the way back! Most Hornets hit ground targets in dive attacks after identifying them visually. But in airspace defended by modern defence systems this would be courting certain disaster. To try to stay alive RAF Tornados, for example, hug the terrain, preferably at night or in a snow blizzard, whilst keeping IAS over 700 knots. And there is no time to study the target or make a second pass across it.

RAF pilot

Of course, it also helps if we are silent, invisible, and don't show on radar or infrared sensors. That way we may really live to fight on Day 2, provided we never go near an airfield where we can be clobbered in between missions.

F/A-18 pilot

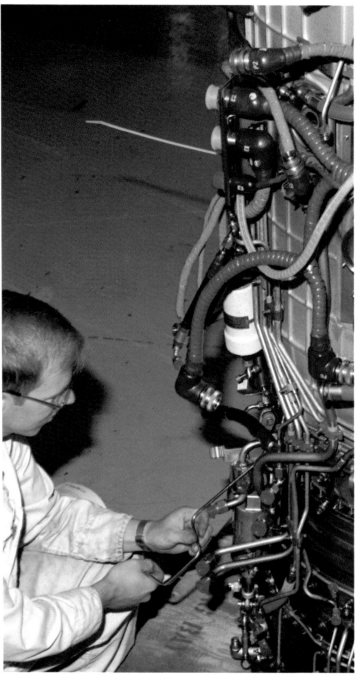

At first, like a lot of guys, I saw complex electronics that seemed to be backups for backups. I pictured a lot of problems. But I changed my mind real quick once I actually got to work on 'em. Follow the regular maintenance tasks – the tests are built-in, so it's a breeze – and your troubleshooting time gets cut down to a third of what it used to be.

Member of F/A-18 maintenance team

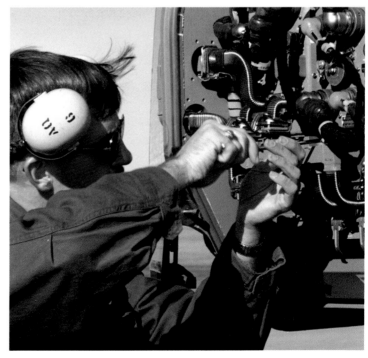

The pilots have their war going on upstairs. Maintenance crews have our own war down on the deck trying to get all these planes turned and off the pointy end. It's a tough test for all the aircraft. They're asking us to keep 'em up about 35 hours a day. But the Hornet does its duty just beautifully. But of course we're specialists. Some of us are qualified to work on the Hughes APG-65 radar; others might crank in another 570 rounds of 20 mike mike.

Hornet avionics engineer

Some guy tried to kid me the Hornet designers put that giant LEX (leading-edge extension) on for reasons of aerodynamics and flight control, especially at high-alpha. We know better, of course. It was put there just to provide some place to fold away the self-contained ladder! On the A-6 you have a kind of fold-down stairway, and on the A-7 you get ropes and crampons and scale up the sheer face of the Eiger, but this Hornet ladder is something else. And it folds away at the touch of a button.

F/A-18 pilot

At McDonnell Douglas we make missiles well as airplanes. The biggest of our tactical missiles is the AGM-84 Harpoon. This can be fired from submarines and surface warships, but it seems to go especially well on our own F/A-18. It gives this small airplane a knock-out punch against enemy ships, and at the same time usefully extends the radius of action. You wouldn't often want to carry two Harpoons (though you can carry four), so to balance the lateral trim, it's handy to hang an AGM-88 HARM, high-speed anti-radiation missile, under the left wing. All that's in addition to the self-defence Sparrows and Sidewinders.

One of the challenges facing the McDonnell/Northrop engineers, in developing the Hornet, is to equip it to fly almost every mission for almost every customer. The Swiss, for example, are quite likely to want to make high-speed passes over hostile armour, destroying tanks with bomblet dispensers or large rockets. The Marines are much more interested in supporting friendly "Grunts" storming a beach than in sending cruise missiles over the horizon. And everyone expects the Hornet to act as an air-combat fighter.

MCAIR spokesman

We're proud of flying the Hornet. We're proud of not being just an F or an A but the new breed of FA squadrons. We can fly fighter and attack in one mission; nobody else can. And we think we can do both missions better. We're also proud that the Hornets don't need the big decks. Here in the Med we were sitting there in April 1986 with three carriers. Ours was *Coral Sea*, by far the smallest deck, but we reckon we did the biggest job when we flew the strike against Tripoli. We had planes from VMFA-314 "Black Knights", VMFA-323 "Death Rattlers", VFA-131 "Wildcats" and VFA-132 "Privateers". There just aren't any more experienced people anywhere, and we did it all off the smallest deck.

F/A-18 pilot

It was expected that the Spanish designation for the Hornet would be C.18, but the number actually chosen is C.15. The 60 single-seat C.15s are tasked mainly with ground attack, though pilots also fly interception missions under the control of the Combate Grande air defence network.

This is the fourth C.15 for the 12th Wing at Torrejón, outside Madrid, which previously flew the C.12 (Phantom). The other Hornet wing, the 15th, based at Zaragoza, has two-seat CE.15 trainers.

MCAIR sales executive

We took a leaf out of the art books of Keith Ferris and painted a false canopy on the underside of our CF-18s. Such simple dodges really do make quite a difference between winning or losing in a close visual air combat. But several of us went to the 1989 Paris airshow, along with one of our airplanes, and when we'd had a good look round the Flanker, which is really the Sukhoi Su-27, we were pretty impressed. Then, when we saw Comrade Evgeny Frolov demonstrate the same airplane, we thought maybe we'd have to do a bit better than just paint false canopies. No way can we flick a CF-18 up on its back to an alpha of 120° and fire accurately into impossible places. What really worried us was that Sukhoi designer Simonov said: "The Su-27 is quite an old aircraft, perhaps we'll be able to show something newer in two years' time".

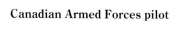

Canadian Armed Forces pilot

Working the Airshow circuit is the other side of the coin. We do a lot of demonstrations which show both the aircraft's and the pilot's capabilities to the full. On the ground we're always in attendance with the plane trying to answer questions – its amazing how informed some people are about the plane you fly.

At big shows we may be away from base for four or five days on others its only a day . . . you just gas up and go home. Each attendance is slightly different but its fun. I enjoy it.

Canadian Armed Forces CF-18 pilot

We've delivered 800 Hornets and have about the same number still to build – though customers keep asking for more. But you can't sit on your hands. We've spent many months trying to put together a big international program for Hornet 2000. We can't do it by ourselves, but with partners this could be as big a program as the original Hornet. It could have any of five configurations, with various upgraded F404 engines of up to 20,000-lb thrust, upgraded avionics, extra fuel in a humpy dorsal tank or in a spliced-in fuselage section, various enlarged tail surfaces and, in the most complete change, a cranked-arrow wing with canard foreplanes. It's not easy, and the Russians are giving competition we didn't expect, but out of it all we hope there'll be a real Super Hornet.

MCAIR executive